KT-420-682

Alfie

Words by Hal David
Music by Burt Bacharach

© Copyright 1966 Famous Music Corporation, USA.
All Rights Reserved. International Copyright Secured.

Music To Watch Girls By
...And More

This publication is not authorised for sale in the United States of America and/or Canada.

Wise Publications
London/New York/Sydney/Paris/Copenhagen/Madrid/Tokyo

DONCASTER LIBRARY SERVICE

30122 01909377 8

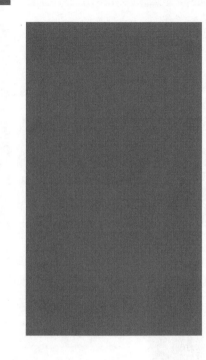

Exclusive distributors:
Music Sales Limited
8/9 Frith Street, London W1V 5TZ, England.
Music Sales Pty Limited
120 Rothschild Avenue, Rosebery, NSW 2018, Australia.

Order No. AM963006
ISBN 0-7119-8043-8
This book © Copyright 1999 by Wise Publications.

Unauthorised reproduction of any part of
this publication by any means including photocopying
is an infringement of copyright.

Printed in the United Kingdom by
Caligraving Limited, Thetford, Norfolk.

Your Guarantee of Quality:
As publishers, we strive to produce every book to
the highest commercial standards.
The book has been carefully designed to minimise awkward
page turns and to make playing from it a real pleasure.
Particular care has been given to specifying acid-free,
neutral-sized paper made from pulps which have not been
elemental chlorine bleached.
This pulp is from farmed sustainable forests and
was produced with special regard for the environment.
Throughout, the printing and binding have been planned
to ensure a sturdy, attractive publication which should
give years of enjoyment.
If your copy fails to meet our high standards,
please inform us and we will gladly replace it.

Music Sales' complete catalogue describes
thousands of titles and is available in full colour sections
by subject, direct from Music Sales Limited.
Please state your areas of interest and send a
cheque/postal order for £1.50 for postage to:
Music Sales Limited, Newmarket Road,
Bury St. Edmunds, Suffolk IP33 3YB.

www.musicsales.com

DONCASTER LIBRARY AND
INFORMATION SERVICE

019093778

MUSIC EXCH 20.11.01

780.2 MUS

Almost There

Words & Music by Jerry Keller & Gloria Shayne

Al - most there, we're al - most there. How won - der - ful,

won - der - ful our love will be for you, for

© Copyright 1964 September Music Corporation & Lynn Hatch Music Company, USA.
The International Music Network Limited, Independent House, 54 Larkshall Road, Chingford, London E4.
All Rights Reserved. International Copyright Secured.

Can't Help Falling In Love

Words & Music by George Weiss, Hugo Peretti & Luigi Creatore

© Copyright 1961 Gladys Music, USA.
Manor Music Company Limited, Iron Bridge House, 3 Bridge Approach, London NW1 for the United Kingdom, Eire,
Israel & the British Dominions, Colonies, Overseas Territories & Dependencies (excluding Canada, Australia and New Zealand).
All Rights Reserved. International Copyright Secured.

love with you. Shall I

stay would it be a

sin if I can't help fall-ing in

love with you. Like a ri-ver flows

Fever

Words & Music by John Davenport & Eddie Cooley

Moderate jump beat

(snap fingers) *(etc.)*

Verse

Am

1. Nev-er know how much I love you.   Nev-er know how much___ I
2. Sun lights up the day-time,   moon lights up___ the
(Verses 3, 4 & 5 see block lyric)

care.
night.

When you put your arms a - round me,   I get a
I light up when you call my name,   and you

© Copyright 1956 Fort Knox Music Company Incorporated & Trio Music Company Incorporated, USA.
Lark Music Limited, Iron Bridge House, 3 Bridge Approach, London NW1 for the British Commonwealth
(excluding Canada & Australasia), Eire and Israel.
All Rights Reserved. International Copyright Secured.

Chorus
N.C.

fe - ver that's so hard ____ to bear.
know I'm gon - na treat ____ you right. } You give me fe - ver

when you kiss me, fe - ver when you hold ____ me

tight. Fe - ver in the morn - ing,

1, 2, 3, 4, 5.

fe - ver all through ____ the night.

Interlude - after 2nd Verse only

Ev - 'ry - bo - dy's

got the fe - ver, that is some - thing you all know.

Fe - ver is - n't such a new thing, fe - ver start - ed long _ a - go.

Verse 3: Romeo loved Juliet Juliet, she felt the same When he put his arms around her, he said "Julie, baby you're my flame."	*Verse 4:* Captain Smith and Pocahontas Had a very mad affair When her Daddy tried to kill him, she said "Daddy-o, don't you dare."
Chorus: Thou givest fever, when we kisseth Fever with thy flaming youth Fever, I'm afire Fever, yea I burn forsooth.	*Chorus:* Give me fever, with his kisses Fever when he holds me tight Fever, I'm his Missus Oh Daddy won't you treat him right.

Verse 5: Now you've listened to my story
Here's the point that I have made
Chicks were born to give you fever
Be it Fahrenheit or Centigrade.

Chorus: They give you fever, when you kiss them
Fever if you live and learn
Fever, till you sizzle
What a lovely way to burn.

Fly Me To The Moon (In Other Words)

Words & Music by Bart Howard

© Copyright 1954 (renewed 1962 & 1973) Almanac Music Incorporated, USA.
TRO Essex Music Limited, Suite 2.07, Plaza 535 Kings Road, London SW10 for the world
(excluding the USA and Canada).
All Rights Reserved. International Copyright Secured.

Mars, in oth-er words, _____ hold my hand, _____ _____ in oth-er words, _____ dar-ling kiss me. _____ _____ Fill my heart with song and let me sing for-ev-er-more. You are all I long for, all I wor-ship and a-

I Left My Heart In San Francisco

Words by Douglas Cross
Music by George Cory

© Copyright 1954 General Music Publishing Company Incorporated, USA.
Dash Music Company Limited, 8/9 Frith Street, London W1.
All Rights Reserved. International Copyright Secured.

climb half-way to the stars, _____ the morn-ing

fog _____ may chill the air, I don't

care! My love was there in San Fran-

cis-co, _____ a-bove the blue _____

— and wind - y sea. When I come

home to you San Fran - cis - co,

your gold - en sun will shine for

1.
me! _____ I left my

2.
me! _____

rall.

MacArthur Park

Words & Music by Jimmy Webb

Spring was nev-er wait-ing for us,
I re-call the yel-low cot-ton

girl, it ran one step a-head as we fol-lowed in the
dress foam-ing like a wave on the ground a-round your

© Copyright 1968 Canopy Music Incorporated, USA.
Universal Music Publishing Limited, 77 Fulham Palace Road, London W6.
All Rights Reserved. International Copyright Secured.

Mac - Ar-thur's Park is melt-ing   in the dark,   all the sweet green ic-ing

flow - ing down.＿＿ Some-one left the cake out in the rain; I don't＿

think that I ＿ can take ＿ it 'cause it took so long to bake it and I'll nev-er have that rec-i-pe a -

gain, oh, no.＿＿＿＿ Oh,＿ no,＿＿＿＿

No, no, no, oh, no.＿

cresc.   rit.   ff

Magic Moments

Words by Hal David
Music by Burt Bacharach

© Copyright 1957 Casa David Music Incorporated & Famous Music Corporation (50%), USA.
Universal/MCA Music Limited, 77 Fulham Palace Road, London W6 (50%).
All Rights Reserved. International Copyright Secured.

rase   the   mem - 'ry   of   these   mag - ic

mo - ments   filled   with   love.

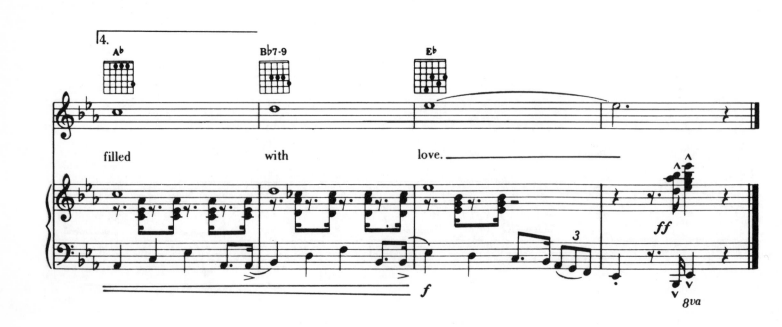

filled   with   love.

Mambo Italiano

Words & Music by Bob Merrill

© Copyright 1954 Golden Bell Songs, USA.
BMG Music Publishing Limited, Bedford House, 69-79 Fulham High Street, London SW6.
All Rights Reserved. International Copyright Secured.

Memories Are Made Of This

Words & Music by Terry Gilkyson, Richard Dehr & Frank Miller

© Copyright 1955 EMI Blackwood Music Incorporated, USA.
Montclare Music Company Limited, 8/9 Frith Street, London W1.
All Rights Reserved. International Copyright Secured.

Don't   for - get a small moon - beam___
With   some bless-ings from a - bove___

Fold   in light- ly with a   dream.
Serve   it gen-'rous-ly with   love.___

Your lips   and mine,   Two sips   of wine, Mem - or -
One man,   one wife,   One love   thro' life, Mem - or -

ies are made of   this.___
ies are made of   this.___

To Coda ⊕

Then add the

wed-ding bells, One house where lov-ers dwell, Three lit-tle kids___ For the

fla-vour, _____ Stir care-f'lly thro' the days See how the

D.%. al Coda

fla-vour stays. These are the dreams you will sav - our.

✛ *CODA*

Mem - or - ies are made of this._____

Moon River

Words by Johnny Mercer
Music by Henry Mancini

© Copyright 1961 Famous Music Corporation, USA.
All Rights Reserved. International Copyright Secured.

mak - er, you heart - break - er, wher - ev - er you're

go - in', ___ I'm go - in' ___ your way. Two

drift - ers, off to see the world. There's such a lot of

world to see. ___ We're af -

Joanna

Words & Music by Tony Hatch & Jackie Trent

© Copyright 1968 Welbeck Music Limited/ATV Music Limited.
Sony/ATV Music Publishing (UK) Limited, 10 Great Marlborough Street, London W1.
All Rights Reserved. International Copyright Secured.

a tempo ♩=68

Good-bye you_____ you long lost sum-mer____ leav-ing me_____

_____ be-hind____ you,____ re-peat-ing things for lov-ers that may____ find you,____

I still hang on_____ to ev-'ry word that day_____ you passed my way.____

Jo-an-na, you made the man___ a child a-gain___ so sweet-ly,____

you may re-mem - ber me

and____ change your

mind._____

On The Rebound

By Floyd Cramer

© Copyright 1960 (renewed 1988) Acuff-Rose Music Incorporated, USA.
Acuff-Rose Music Limited, 25 James Street, London W1.
All Rights Reserved. International Copyright Secured.

Something Stupid

Words & Music by C. Carson Parks

© Copyright 1967 Greenwood Music Company, USA.
Montclare Music Limited, 8/9 Frith Street, London W1.
All Rights Reserved. International Copyright Secured.

Then af - ter - wards we drop in - to a
The time is right, your per - fume fills my

qui - et lit - tle place and have a
head, the stars get red, and oh, the

drink or two.
night is so blue.

And

then I go and spoil it all by say - in' some - thin' stu - pid, like "I

To next strain

love you."   I can love you."

See it in your eyes that you de - spise the same old lines you heard the

night be - fore._____ And

though it's just a line to you, for me it's true and nev - er seemed so

right be - fore.

D.S. al Fine %

I

That's Amore (That's Love)

Words by Jack Brooks
Music by Harry Warren

© Copyright 1954 Paramount Music Corporation
& Famous Music Corporation (50%) & Four Jays Music Publishing Company, USA.
Leosong Copyright Service Limited, Independent House, 54 Larkshall Road, Chingford, London E4 (50%).
All Rights Reserved. International Copyright Secured.

mor - é. _____ When the

world seems to shine like you've had too much wine, that's a -

mor - é. _____ Bells will

ring, ting - a - ling - a - ling, ting - a - ling - a - ling, and you'll sing, "Vee - ta

bel - la." _____ Hearts will

play, tip - py - tip - py - tay, tip - py - tip - py - tay like a gay tar - an -

tel - la. _____ (Luck - y fel - la.) When the

stars make you drool just like pas - ta fa - zool, that's a -

mor - é. _____ When you

dance down the street with a cloud at your feet, you're in

love. _____ When you

walk in a dream but you know you're not dream - ing, Sig -

She

Words by Herbert Kretzmer
Music by Charles Aznavour

1. She may be the face I can't for- get, a trace of plea-sure or re- gret, may be my trea-sure or the price I have to pay, she may be the song that sum - mer

© Copyright 1974 Standard Music Limited, 11 Uxbridge Street, London W8.
All Rights Reserved. International Copyright Secured.

sings,_____ may be the chill that au-tumn brings,_____ may be a hun-dred diff-'rent

things_____ with-in the mea-sure of a day.

2. She_____ may be the beau-ty or the beast,_____ may be the fa-mine or the
(Verse 3 instr. Verse 4 see block lyric)

feast,_____ may turn each day in-to a hea-ven or___ hell.

She— may be the mir-ror of my dreams— a smile re-flect-ed in a stream, she may not be what she may

3° To Coda ⊕

seem, in - side her shell.

She— who al-ways seems so hap-py in a crowd,— whose eyes can be so pri-vate and so

proud,— no-one's al-lowed to see them when they cry.

Verse 4:

She may be the reason I survive

The why and wherefore I'm alive

The one I'll care for through the rough and ready years.

Me, I'll take her laughter and her tears

And make them all my souvenirs

For where she goes I've got to be

The meaning of my life is she, she, she.

What A Wonderful World

Words & Music by George David Weiss & Bob Thiele

© Copyright 1967 Range Road Music Incorporated, Quartet Music Incorporated & Abilene Music Incorporated, USA.
Carlin Music Corporation, Iron Bridge House, 3 Bridge Approach, London NW1 (50%)
& Memory Lane Music Limited, 22 Denmark Street, London WC2 (50%).
All Rights Reserved. International Copyright Secured.

Wichita Lineman

Words & Music by Jimmy Webb

© Copyright 1968 Canopy Music Incorporated, USA.
Universal Music Publishing Limited, 77 Fulham Palace Road, London W6.
All Rights Reserved. International Copyright Secured.

Wives And Lovers

Words by Hal David
Music by Burt Bacharach

© Copyright 1963 Famous Music Corporation, USA.
All Rights Reserved. International Copyright Secured.

you need-n't try an-y more._____ For wives should

al-ways be lov-ers too. Run to his

arms_____ the mo-ment he_____ comes home to you. I'm warn-ing

you._____ Day af-ter day there are

girls at the of-fice and men will al-ways be men. ____ Don't send him off with your hair still in curl-ers, You may not see him a-gain, ____ for wives should al-ways be lov-ers

More great music titles arranged for piano, voice and guitar...for you!

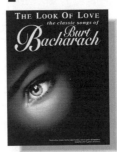

The Look Of Love:
The Classic Songs Of Burt Bacharach.
Twenty-three all-time classic hits from the master songwriter, arranged for piano, complete with guitar chord boxes and lyrics. Includes '(They Long To Be) Close To You', 'Twenty-Four Hours From Tulsa' and 'The Look Of Love'.
AM937475

The Great Songs Of The Carpenters
Fourteen classic love songs from one of the most successful recording acts of the 70s. Includes 'We've Only Just Begun' and 'Hurting Each Other'.
AM39108

The Best Of Patsy Cline
A dozen memorable songs from one of the greats of country and western. Arranged for piano, voice and guitar, complete with lyrics and guitar chord boxes.
AM82454

Neil Diamond: The Greatest Hits 1966-1992
Thirty-seven of Neil Diamond's greatest songs. Includes 'Beautiful Noise', 'Song Sung Blue', 'Love On The Rocks' and 'You Don't Bring Me Flowers'.
AM90292

Marlene Dietrich: The Songbook
Fourteen songs immortalised by the legendary Marlene Dietrich, transcribed from the original sheet music editions. Features a unique folio of portraits and contemporary studio photographs, and includes a special introduction and background notes on each song. Songs include the classic, 'Falling In Love Again' and 'Honeysuckle Rose'.
AM950389

Ella Fitzgerald: The Memorial Album
Fifteen all-time favourites in full arrangements for piano, voice and guitar. Includes 'The Lady Is A Tramp', 'Can't Help Loving 'Dat Man' and 'I'm Getting Sentimental Over You'.
AM940093

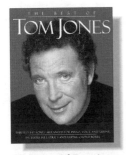

The Best Of Tom Jones
Thirteen hit songs arranged for piano, voice and guitar. Includes 'It's Not Unusual', 'What's new Pussy Cat', 'Delilah' and 'The Green, Green Grass Of Home'.
AM951786

The Essential Jerome Kern Songbook
The definitive Jerome Kern songbook, containing all his best songs arranged for piano, voice and guitar. Includes 'The Last Time I Saw Paris', 'They Didn't Believe Me', 'The Song Is You' and 'Long Ago And Far Away'.
AM81506

The Peggy Lee Songbook
Eighteen of her greatest hits including 'Fever', 'Just One Of Those Things', 'Big Spender, 'He's A Tramp' and 'I'm A Woman'.
AM945054

Marilyn Sings!:
The Marilyn Monroe Songbook
A superb folio presenting many songs as featured by screen goddess Marilyn Monroe. Includes 'Some Like It Hot', 'A Fine Romance', 'That Old Black Magic', 'Bye-Bye Baby' and 'My Heart Belongs To Daddy'.
AM85341

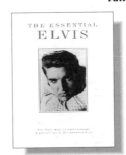

Elvis Presley: The Essential Elvis
The very best of Elvis Presley, newly arranged for piano, voice and guitar with full lyrics and chords symbols. Includes 'Jailhouse Rock', 'All Shook Up' and 'Wooden Heart'.
AM927872

The Frank Sinatra Anthology
The definitive collection...58 classic Sinatra songs arranged for piano, voice and guitar. Includes 'Come Fly With Me', 'The Lady Is A Tramp' and 'My Way'.
AM939455

Even more fantastic compilations, classic songs & great melodies...for you!

After Midnight: Blues
Thirty-two sophisticated blues numbers to match the romantic mood. Includes 'Smoke gets In Your Eyes', 'That Ole Devil Called Love', 'Strangers In The Night' and 'Angel Eyes'.
AM951742

After Midnight: Jazz
Thirty-one sophisticated jazz numbers to match the romantic mood. Includes 'Lullaby Of Birdland', 'Stella By Starlight', 'The Night We Called It A Day' and 'These Foolish Things'.
AM951753

The All-Time Greatest Love Songs
Thirty-two of the world's favourite love songs - a stunning collection including 'What Can I Do' (The Corrs), 'Can You Feel The Love Tonight' (Elton John) and 'Save The Best For Last' (Vanessa Williams).
AM957900

The All-Time Greatest Movie Songs
Classic tracks from some of the most popular films of the 80s and 90s. Nineteen massive hits including 'Up Where We Belong' from *An Officer And A Gentleman*, 'Love Is All Around' from *Four Weddings And A Funeral* and 'Blaze Of Glory' from *Young Guns II*.
AM957275

An Old Fashioned Love Song
Thirty-five songs of love arranged for voice, piano and guitar. Includes 'And I Love You So', 'Strangers In The Night' and 'Moonglow', complete with lyrics.
AM85382

As Time Goes By
Twenty-six theme songs including 'Till The End Of Time', 'Long Ago And Far Away' and 'the Last Time I Saw Paris'
AM88875

The Essential Songwriters Collection
Three superb folios of music by the greats of the golden age...*The Essential George Gershwin*...in piano solo arrangements. *The Essential Jerome Kern*... in piano/vocal arrangements. *The Essential Duke Ellington*...in piano/vocal arrangements. Slipcase edition.
AM92312

Stage & Screen: The Black Book
Fifty great songs including 'A Certain Smile', 'Bright Eyes', 'Live And Let Die', 'Sunrise, Sunset' and 'Thank Heaven For Little Girls'.
AM92249

Stage & Screen: The White Book
Words and music to all-time hits from the world's favourite movies and musicals. Includes 'From Russia With Love', 'Pennies From Heaven', 'Where Is Love?', 'Hello Dolly' and 'Jailhouse Rock'.
AM92248

Available from all good music retailers or, in case of difficulty, direct from
**Music Sales Limited, Newmarket Road, Bury St. Edmunds, Suffolk IP33 3YP.
Telephone 01284 725725; Fax 01284 702592.**
See also page 2 for details of Music Sales' complete colour catalogues!
www. musicsales.com